The Prophets of Allah

Volume I
Elementary Level

Suhaib Hamid Ghazi

Illustrated by Mike Rezac and Jennifer Mazzoni

 IQRA' International Educational Foundation

Part of a Comprehensive and Systematic Program of Islamic Studies

**An Enrichment Book
in the Program of Sirah
Elementary Level**

Approved By
Rabita al-Alam al-Islami
Makkah Mukarramah

Chief Program Editors
Abidullah al-Ansari Ghazi
(PhD Harvard University)

Tasneema Ghazi
(PhD University of Minnesota)

Language Editors
Hina Azam
Suhaib Hamid Ghazi
Huda Quraishi

Designers
Jennifer Mazzoni
(B.A. Illustration,
Columbia College Chicago)

Laura Boyce
(B.F.A. Graphic Design,
University of Illinois at Chicago)

Redesign
Sabeehuddin Khaja

IQRA'S NOTE

We, at IQRA' International Educational Foundation, are grateful to Allah (SWT) for enabling us to present the first volume of The Prophets of Allah for our young readers. The present volume contains the life and the teachings of the four early prophets of Allah (SWT) as mentioned in the Qur'an and the Hadith. Four more volumes containing the life and the teachings of the Prophets mentioned in the Qur'an will soon follow, *InshaAllah*.

These books are part of IQRA's comprehensive and systematic program of Islamic education. We wish to introduce our young children to the enriched field of Islamic Social Studies through the stories and teachings of the Prophets of Allah (SWT). This is the beginning of a comprehensive study and understanding of the role of human beings as the Khalifah of Allah on this planet.

The stories are incorporated in IQRA's curriculum of Islamic history (Social Studies) at the Kindergarten level. It is recommended that the teachers should consult and study the curriculum guide for daily lesson planning and teachings. However, the stories are independent enough to be read to the young non-readers in informal settings. Second and third graders will enjoy reading these books on their own as the readability level of these stories is appropriate for them.

The Prophets of Allah series is the part of IQRA's comprehensive and systematic program of Islamic education which covers:

1. An integrated Curriculum from pre-school to high school.

2. A comprehensive program of Islamic studies at each level (pre-school — high school) to include ten basic Islamic subjects and to cover graded textbooks, workbooks, enrichment literature, parents'/teachers' manuals and educational aids.

We urge all concerned Muslims and Islamic organizations to cooperate with IQRA' and become an ANSAR of its educational program. We believe that together we can succeed, *InshaAllah*.

Dedication

I would like to dedicate this book to my loving parents
for the knowledge and love they have
given to me throughout my life,
and for the sincerity and dedication with which they work
to achieve quality Islamic education in America.

May Allāh ﷻ bless them and their efforts.

CONTENTS

	Page
The Prophet Ādam ﷺ	*3*
The Prophet Nūh ﷺ	*21*
The Prophet Hūd ﷺ	*43*
The Prophet Ṣālih ﷺ	*55*

The Story of Creation

and the Beginning of Man

Before there was anything else, there was Allah ﷻ. Then Allah ﷻ decided to create the universe we know. Allah ﷻ created the stars, the sun, the moon, and all the planets, including the Earth.

On Earth, he created all of the oceans, forests, mountains, rivers, trees and flowers. Then Allah ﷻ wanted to create a man, and so He did. He called the man Adam – the first man ever.

Adam ﷺ was not like the other creations on Earth. He was a very special creation of Allah ﷻ. Allah gave him a mind with which he could think and choose. He gave him a heart in order that he may feel and love. Allah ﷻ "Put onto him His own spirit." (15:29) Allah ﷻ gave Adam ﷺ a special place to live called Jannah. Jannah means "garden." Adam had everything that he needed in Jannah, and he was very happy living there.

THE DISOBEDIENCE OF IBLIS

Allah's special gift to Adam ﷺ was the gift of knowledge. He taught Adam ﷺ many things. He taught him the names of "all things." He gave Adam ﷺ a desire to learn. None of Allah's ﷻ creations knew as much as Adam ﷺ did, not even His angels. He was very special to Allah ﷻ.

One day, Allah ﷻ asked the angels and the jinn to come and see Adam ﷺ, His new creation. When everyone gathered, Allah ﷻ asked the angels to tell Him the names of some of His creations. The angels could not answer the questions. They said, "O, Allah ﷻ, we know only what you have taught us. You are perfect in knowledge and wisdom." (2:32) The angels did not know the names of those things.

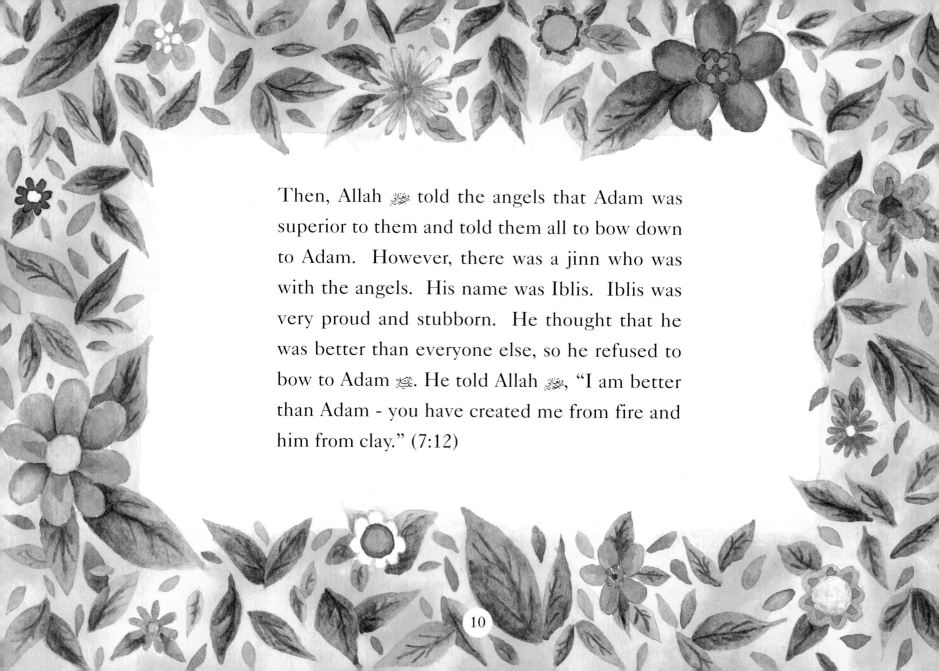

Then, Allah ﷻ told the angels that Adam was superior to them and told them all to bow down to Adam. However, there was a jinn who was with the angels. His name was Iblis. Iblis was very proud and stubborn. He thought that he was better than everyone else, so he refused to bow to Adam ﷺ. He told Allah ﷻ, "I am better than Adam - you have created me from fire and him from clay." (7:12)

Allah ﷻ is kind and merciful, but He does not like disobedience. Allah ﷻ was angry at Iblis and made him leave Jannah. Iblis had no choice. He had to leave. Before he left, he told Allah ﷻ that he would make Adam عليه السلام and all his children disobey Allah ﷻ. Allah ﷻ said he could try, but the good people of Allah would never listen to him. (7:11-15)

ADAM ﷺ, HAWWA ﷺ
AND THE FORBIDDEN FRUIT

Allah ﷻ created all creatures on Earth in pairs. Allah ﷻ created another human being along with Adam ﷺ, a woman named Hawwa ﷺ. She was a beautiful and noble woman. Adam ﷺ and Hawwa ﷺ lived in Jannah. They were both happy there. Allah ﷻ gave them everything that they wanted.

Allah ﷻ told Adam ﷺ and Hawwa ﷻ to eat any of the fruits and vegetables in Heaven, except for the fruits of one tree. Adam ﷺ and Hawwa ﷻ were very careful to keep away from this forbidden tree. They wanted to obey Allah ﷻ.

However, Iblis did not like Adam ﷺ and Hawwa ﷻ. He thought it was Adam's ﷺ fault that Allah had sent him away. He wanted to get Adam ﷺ and Hawwa ﷻ kicked out of Heaven, just like he had been. So he kept trying to make them disobey Allah ﷻ. He told them if they ate the fruit of the forbidden tree, they would live forever. Finally one day, Adam ﷺ and Hawwa ﷻ both decided to eat the fruit. They disobeyed Allah's ﷻ commands.

As soon as they tasted it, they both felt very sorry that they had listened to Iblis. They tried to hide in the woods and cover themselves. They felt very ashamed and did not want Allah to see them.

But Allah ﷻ sees everything, and He knew what they had done. He ordered them both to leave Jannah. Jannah is only for those who obey Allah ﷻ. Allah ﷻ sent Adam ﷺ and Hawwa ﷂ down to Earth. They were both very sad to leave Jannah, but they knew they were both responsible for disobeying Allah ﷻ.

Adam ﷺ and Hawwa ﷂ cried and begged

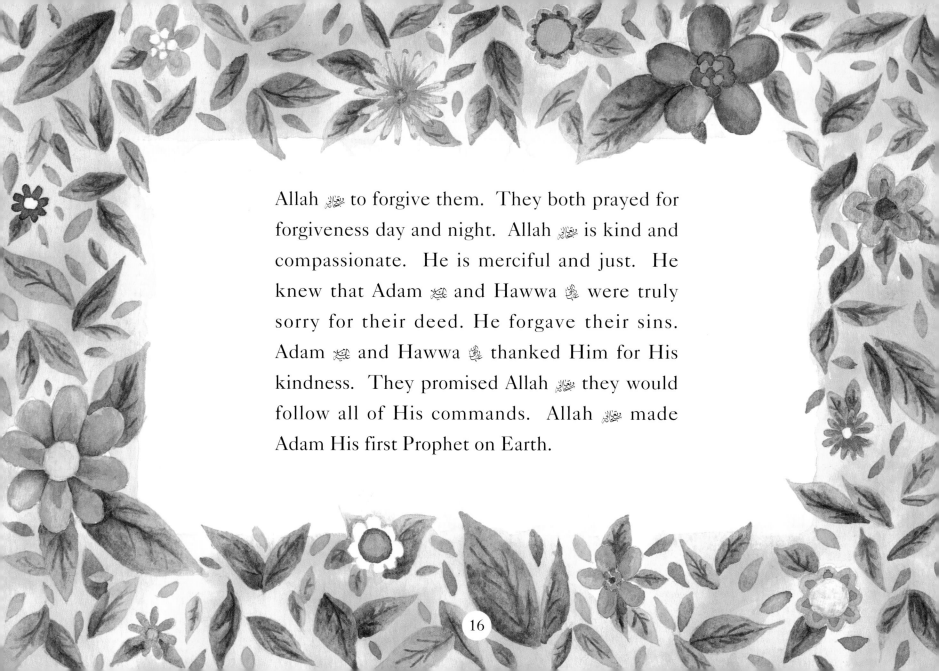

Allah ﷻ to forgive them. They both prayed for forgiveness day and night. Allah ﷻ is kind and compassionate. He is merciful and just. He knew that Adam ﷺ and Hawwa ﵂ were truly sorry for their deed. He forgave their sins. Adam ﷺ and Hawwa ﵂ thanked Him for His kindness. They promised Allah ﷻ they would follow all of His commands. Allah ﷻ made Adam His first Prophet on Earth.

Allah ﷻ promised to guide Adam ﷺ and those after him, so that those who followed His guidance could return to Jannah after their life here on Earth.

Iblis remained their enemy. He and his children are still our enemies. Anyone who urges us to disobey Allah ﷻ is a friend of Iblis, and we must never listen to him. Iblis always tries to keep us away from Jannah, and his promises are never true.

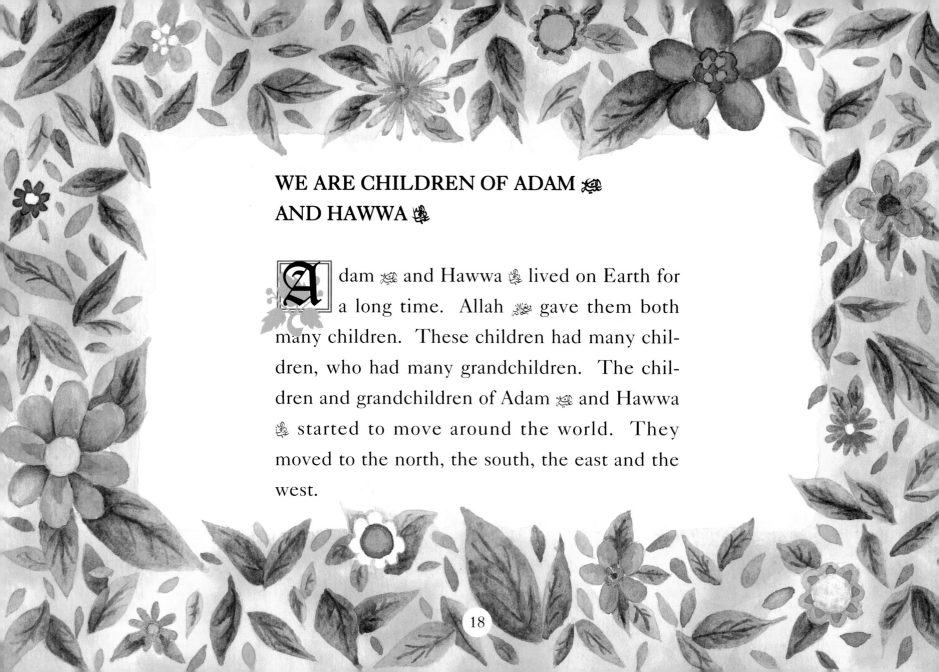

WE ARE CHILDREN OF ADAM ﷺ AND HAWWA ﷺ

Adam ﷺ and Hawwa ﷺ lived on Earth for a long time. Allah ﷻ gave them both many children. These children had many children, who had many grandchildren. The children and grandchildren of Adam ﷺ and Hawwa ﷺ started to move around the world. They moved to the north, the south, the east and the west.

We are all children of Adam ﷺ and Hawwa ﷺ. This means that we are all brothers and sisters. The whole world is one big family, and that is why we should try to live in peace and harmony – just like a family.

Prophet Nuh

'Alaihi-(a)ṣ-Salām

Long, long ago in the land of Mesopotamia, there was a town of people who lived wild and evil lives. Even though their ancestors had been good Muslims, they no longer believed in Islam. Instead, they prayed to idols which they made themselves. They would decorate wood and stone idols and ask them for everything they desired.

The chiefs and leaders of the town were very wealthy people. They were rude and arrogant, and they thought of nothing but money. They controlled the town, and the poor people lived in fear of them and their evil ways.

Allah ﷻ was very angry with the wealthy people in the community. He had blessed them with wealth, land and beautiful houses, but they didn't thank Him or share it with the poor people. This was wrong.

So Allah ﷻ decided to send them a messenger to teach them Islam, like their ancestors had been taught.

Allah ﷻ felt that the best way to turn the unfaithful people to the goodness of Islam was to send them a person from among themselves. He knew that the people would pay more attention to a person they knew than to a stranger.

Allah ﷻ chose a man named Nuh ﷺ.

Nuh ﷺ was a very humble and gentle man. He was pious and kind, and he always spoke the truth. He was so trustworthy and wise that people would come to him for advice.

His reputation as a truthful and gentle person helped him when he was chosen to be a Prophet, and he gained a few followers. All of his followers were poor people, because the wealthy people were too proud to listen to what Prophet Nuh ﷺ has to say.

Prophet Nuh ﷺ told his people, "Worship only Allah ﷻ. There is no God but Him. Otherwise, I fear that you will see the punishment of a painful day." (7:59)

The chiefs of the people laughed at Prophet Nuh ﷺ. One of their leaders stepped forth and said, "You are nothing but a man like ourselves. We don't see anything special about you. You have only a few followers and they are the poorest and the lowest from among us. We do not think that you are better than we are. In fact, we think you are a liar!" (11:27) The chiefs thought that just because they had a lot of money, they were better than Prophet Nuh ﷺ and his

followers. They used this as an excuse not to believe in Islam.

Prophet Nuh ﷺ said, "I have been sent with a message of mercy, but if you refuse to see the truth in it, I cannot force you to accept it. Oh, my people! I do not ask you for your wealth, for my reward will come from Allah ﷻ." (11:28-29) Prophet Nuh ﷺ made it clear that he didn't want the people's money, and that neither he nor Allah ﷻ was impressed by how much money a person had. He told them "I will never turn away a believer who has little money. I will never tell my poor followers that Allah ﷻ will not reward them. Surely, Allah ﷻ knows best what is in their hearts. I see that you are very ignorant people."

The leaders of the town became upset and angry because Prophet Nuh ﷺ had made a very good point. One of them finally said, "O, Nuh! You have argued with us so many times and we still don't care what you say. We don't believe you. If what you say is true, then bring upon us the punishment you warn us about!" (11:32)

Prophet Nuh ﷺ calmly replied, "Only Allah ﷻ will bring the punishment upon you, and when he does, there will be no

escape. None of my advice will help you if Allah ﷻ wills that you remain ignorant. Allah ﷻ is your Lord, and to Him you shall return." (11:33-34)

After some time, Allah ﷻ revealed to Prophet Nuh ﷺ that no more people would join him. Allah ﷻ told him not to worry about those who didn't believe. Instead, he should make plans to build - of all things - an ark! Prophet Nuh ﷺ and his followers knew Allah was wise and powerful. They knew that Allah only commanded what was good for them, even if they didn't understand. And so,

Prophet Nuh ﷺ and his followers quickly began working to build the ark. Building an ark was a big job. An ark was not just an ordinary boat. It was a huge boat. It had to be strong enough to carry everything Allah wanted to put in it. Prophet Nuh ﷺ and his people worked hard. They used long, wooden planks and nailed them together. They worked for many, many days under the hot sun, which burned like a bright lamp in the middle of the clear desert sky.

Sometimes the townsfolk would walk by and make fun of Prophet Nuh ﷺ and

his people. They would say, "You must be crazy to build an ark in the middle of the desert. There is no sea in this area! Do you plan to sail on the sand? Maybe you will pull the ark across the desert!" The people would point and laugh at Prophet Nuh ﷺ and his followers. Sometimes they threatened to hurt them. Even Prophet Nuh's wife did not agree with him.

Prophet Nuh ﷺ was patient. He would reply "Though you are laughing at us, we are laughing at you in the same manner. You will soon know who will face the punishment of Allah ﷻ."

(11:39) He would then return to building the ark, and he didn't let the people's insults stop him. As they were working Allah was watching them.

By working hard and working together, Prophet Nuh ﷺ and his followers soon finished the ark and waited for Allah's next command. What did Allah ﷻ have in mind?

Allah ﷻ ordered Prophet Nuh ﷺ to gather a male and female of each type of animal and put them in the boat.

He and his followers gathered pairs of
frogs, hippos, bears, sheep, ducks,

ostriches, giraffes, elephants and every animal they could find. Then the pious company loaded the animals in the ark, pair by pair.

Prophet Nuh's ﷺ followers and their children gathered their belongings and boarded the ark.

Prophet Nuh ﷺ and his children, except for one son, boarded the arc after all were aboard.

The sky darkened to black as storm clouds rolled in from all over. The clouds seemed to swallow up the light, and thunder began to boom like cannons. Lightning streaked across the sky like crooked snakes, but when they disappeared, the town was once again under a blanket of darkness.

People came out of their homes and began wondering why it was going to rain after such a long drought. They would soon find out.

Then Allah ﷻ unleashed the storm clouds. Rain came down furiously from the sky. There was so much rain that the ground couldn't absorb it. But it kept pouring, becoming deeper and deeper. Then, water started to gush out from the ground! The people were terrified. There was water coming from everywhere! Where could they go?

As the water level rose, a wind developed and powerful waves crashed all around, crushing the houses and trees like toothpicks.

Some people ran to the mountains and hills, trying to climb higher than the waves. One of Prophet Nuh's sons was among these people. Prophet Nuh ﷺ called for him, "Oh son! Come with us and be safe! Do not die with the non-believers!"

But his son yelled, "I am going to the top of the mountain. I will be safe from the water over there!"

Prophet Nuh ﷺ sadly replied, "Today there is nobody who is safe, except for those on whom Allah ﷻ has mercy."

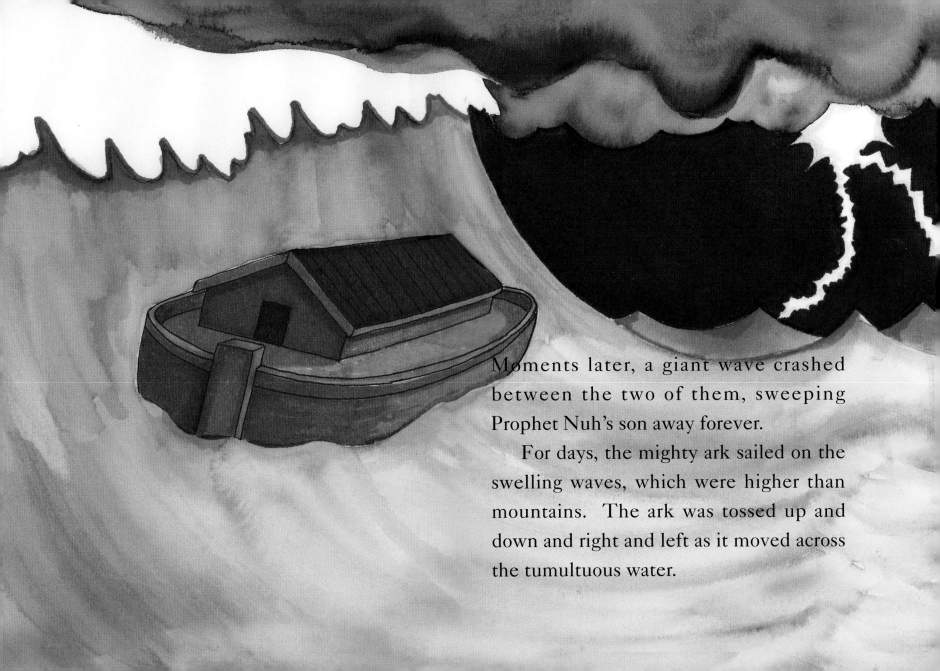

Moments later, a giant wave crashed between the two of them, sweeping Prophet Nuh's son away forever.

For days, the mighty ark sailed on the swelling waves, which were higher than mountains. The ark was tossed up and down and right and left as it moved across the tumultuous water.

Though everyone else had drowned Allah ﷻ kept Prophet Nuh ﷺ and his people safe.

Then Allah gave his commandment. "O Earth; swallow up your water! O sky, be clear of clouds!" (11:44) Allah ﷻ stopped the rain and brought the sun out. The ground swallowed up the water as if there had never been a flood, and the ark came to rest on Mount Judi. Prophet Nuh ﷺ and his brave followers were now safe from the danger of the nonbelievers.

Prophet Nuh ﷺ cried to Allah ﷻ, "Oh Allah! My son is of my family, and now he is dead. Why did you refuse to save him? You are the most just of judges." (11:45-46)

Allah ﷻ replied, "O, Nuh! He is not a part of your household. He was a person of evil conduct. He refused to see the truth. Do not question My decisions on subjects about which you do not know."

It didn't make a difference that he was related to Prophet Nuh ﷺ. Prophet Nuh ﷺ realized what Allah ﷻ was saying and apologized, "My Lord, I seek refuge in you. I am sorry for asking you about a decision you made. You know better than anyone. If you don't forgive me, I shall be amongst the lost people."

Allah ﷻ forgave Prophet Nuh ﷺ and told him to lead his followers and the animals off the ark. Down came Prophet Nuh ﷺ and down came the followers. Then came the animals in pairs. The animals spread out across the land. Some went to the jungle, some went to the forest, some went to the desert, and some went to the mountains. The fish went to the oceans, the sea and the lakes, while the birds flapped their wings and flew to different parts of the Earth.

Prophet Nuh ﷺ and his people came down from the mountain in peace. They prayed together without fear of being beaten or ridiculed. They thanked Allah ﷻ for saving them and wept with tears of joy. They knew that now they could start a new life without being bothered by other people. They were free to pray to Allah ﷻ and live as He wanted them to live.

Through time, Prophet Nuh's followers grew in number. They spread out far and wide across the face of the Earth. Many went across land and many went across water. They built new homes and towns wherever they went.

They put *masajid* and schools in these towns to teach the young. For many decades they lived happily and Allah ﷻ sent among them Prophets to keep His Message alive.

Prophet Hud

'Alaihi-(a)ṣ-Salām

The followers of Prophet Nuh ﷺ were noble Muslims who settled down in Arabia and lived pious lives. But, as time went by, some of their children drifted away from the way of Islam. They forgot the guidance of Allah ﷻ and began worshipping idols, drinking alcohol, gambling, and cheating each other.

One group of Nuh's ﷺ descendants was called 'Ad. Instead of Allah ﷻ, the 'Ad prayed to many different idols. They believed that each idol fulfilled a different need.

According to them, all the powers that really belong to Allah ﷻ were divided among these many gods. And instead of worshipping Allah ﷻ alone, they worshipped different gods all at the same time. They believed that their idols had given them everything.

The people of 'Ad were tall, handsome, and strong people. They were excellent architects and skilled engineers. They liked to build castles and magnificent buildings, and they planted beautiful gardens and orchards. But they did not realize that their abilities and the natural resources around them were gifts from Allah ﷻ. In spite of all these gifts from Allah ﷻ, they denied His power. Even though the people of 'Ad were great builders, they had no morals.

In the markets, many would use false weights and measures to cheat people.

The poor people spent all of their money
but still could not get enough to eat.

The rich people kept their wealth to themselves and refused to listen to anybody's advice.

Allah ﷻ chose one man from among them to be a Prophet. This man was named Hud ﷺ. Prophet Hud ﷺ tried to teach the people of 'Ad that there is only one God and that everything - rain and safety and food and health - is from Him. Hud ﷺ told them again and again to stop worshiping their idols. He begged them to live according to Allah's ﷻ will. He warned them about Allah's ﷻ punishment of those who disobeyed Him, and especially for those who worshiped false gods. He told them,

"O my people! I am not asking for any reward from you. I am simply sent by the Lord of the worlds to warn you and call you back to the path of truth and goodness. If you ask forgiveness from Allah ﷻ and change your ways, He will make you stronger than you are now. He will give you plenty of rain. And He will accept you. You must not continue your evil ways."

Most of the people of 'Ad were not ready to listen to Prophet Hud ﷺ. They told him, "You're stupid! You're just telling us old wives' tales. We know that we are not going to be punished and destroyed like the people of Nuh."

However, Prophet Hud ﷺ knew that Allah's ﷻ punishment would come to his people.

After trying to convince them, he decided to leave the valley of Al-Ahqaf with the people who listened to his message and were Muslims.

As soon as Hud ﷺ left the village, a large cloud appeared in the sky. The people of 'Ad were happy to see it, because they thought that it would bring rain to their desert land. Little did they know that Allah ﷻ was sending a terrible wind-storm through the cloud.

The clouds grew larger and larger as the wind howled louder and louder. The air was full of dust and sand. The wind blew so violently that the people ran into their big houses and beautiful castles to hide.

But nothing could save them from the
punishment of Allah ﷻ.

The storm raged for eight days (69:6-7) and seven nights. Their houses were filled with sand and all the people were smothered. Then the wind blew all the sand back across the desert. There was nothing left except the big empty houses of 'Ad, which were useless against the punishment of Allah ﷻ. Their idols could do nothing against His will, and they now were broken and strewn over the dead land.

The only people from 'Ad who were saved from the storm were those who had left with Prophet Hud ﷺ. The children of these believers grew up to become good Muslims who believed in Allah ﷻ alone and lived honest lives.

Prophet Salih ﷺ

and the People of Thamud

'Alaihi-(a)ṣ-Salām

The people of Thamud were the descendants of those people of 'Ad who survived Allah's ﷻ punishment and followed the teachings of their prophet, Prophet Hud ﷺ. They used to live in the valley of Qura, which is located in Arabia. Today, it is called Fajjul-Naqa.

Allah ﷻ gave many comforts to the people of Thamud. They were blessed with "lush" or "colorful" gardens, lovely flowers and rich orchards filled with all kinds of fruits. A great river of clear, clean water flowed through the valley, and graceful, tall mountains surrounded it.

The people of Thamud were beautiful and strong people. Allah ﷻ had given them a special gift. He had made them skillful builders and planners. They used their skills to carve beautiful houses and buildings out of the mountains. They could cut and shape the mountain stone like it was clay. The people of Thamud were famous for their stone carvings and architecture. People from far away would come to visit their beautiful city.

But as time passed, the people of Thamud forgot the teachings of both Prophet Hud ﷺ and Prophet Nuh ﷺ before him. They became arrogant and proud. They began to believe that they were the most powerful people on earth, and that they could do anything that they wanted.

They forgot that everything is created by Allah ﷻ and that He is most powerful. They did not believe that if Allah ﷻ wanted, He could destroy everything, including their city, with all of its marvelous buildings and lovely gardens.

The people of Thamud began to think they were going to live forever. They became ignorant and began to worship idols instead of Allah ﷻ alone. They made many different idols, gave them

names and started bowing in front of them. They asked them for everything they needed and worshiped them as their gods.

At this time, Allah ﷻ decided to send a prophet to teach these people, just like He had sent one to the people of Prophet Nuh ﷺ and Prophet Hud ﷺ.

Allah ﷻ sent Prophet Salih ﷺ to the people of Thamud. Prophet Salih was a noble and pious man. Everyone knew him for his good nature and intelligence. He respected his elders and loved the young. He was helpful to those around him. His father was very proud of Salih ﷺ and thought that his son would grow up to be a rich man. However, Allah ﷻ had a different plan for Prophet Salih ﷺ.

Allah ﷻ wanted Prophet Salih ﷺ to bring his people out of the darkness of their beliefs. He asked Prophet Salih ﷺ to teach the people of Thamud to worship only Allah ﷻ.

Prophet Salih ﷺ told his people that he was the messenger of Allah ﷻ and that Allah had sent him to teach them about the right path. Prophet Salih told his people that he was their brother and their friend and that whatever he was telling them was for their own good. He told them to give up their bad habits of cheating, lying, drinking and idol worship, and asked them to listen to his message. He told everybody in the valley, "There is no God but Allah ﷻ. He is the only one that we should worship. He has created us and settled us on this earth. We should ask Him for help." (11:61)

There were a small number of people who believed in Prophet Salih's ﷺ teachings and became his followers. But most of them did not want to pay any attention to his message. They refused to change their evil ways. Some people of Thamud thought that Prophet Salih ﷺ was a magician and that they were not going to listen to him unless he brought some special sign, proving that he was sent by Allah ﷻ.

Prophet Salih ﷺ asked them, "What sign do you want to see?"

One of them replied, "If you are a true Prophet, Salih, then make a camel appear from underneath this mountain!"

"Yes," said another, "and then make her deliver a baby camel as soon as she comes out!" The crowd laughed. They thought that a camel could never come out of the mountain, because a camel can only be born from its mother. They wanted to make a fool out of Prophet Salih ﷺ. They thought that if he failed, then he would feel ashamed and stop telling people to worship only Allah ﷻ.

The people of Thamud were not aware of Allah's power. They did not know that if Allah wants to do anything, then He does it right away. Nothing is impossible for Allah ﷻ, as He has power over everything and everyone. Prophet Salih ﷺ had faith in Allah's ﷻ power, so he prayed to Him and said, "O Allah, show them whatever they want to see."

Allah  heard Prophet Salih's prayer. Immediately, the mountain opened, and a camel came out.

She delivered a baby as soon as she came out of the mountain. The people were shocked, and it took them some time to believe their eyes.

Prophet Salih ﷺ told the people that the camel was a sign from Allah ﷻ and that they had to protect her and share the water and grass with her. They agreed to let the mother camel drink the water from the well every other day. Their animals would leave the well water alone on those days. But the people of Thammad did not really want to believe Prophet Salih's message, and even the miracle of the camel could not convince them. Most of the people thought that Prophet Salih had played a trick on them, and they went on rejecting his message.

There were some cruel people who did not like the mother camel at all. Even though they had promised to help protect the mother camel, they wanted to kill her. One day they actually did. When Prophet Salih ﷺ found out the people had broken their promise, he felt sad and angry. He warned his people about Allah's ﷻ punishment. He told them, "You are unfortunate people because you could not be patient. You disobeyed Allah ﷻ. Now you will

receive his punishment. After three days, the punishment will come and destroy all of you."

Prophet Salih ﷺ and his followers packed their belongings and prepared to leave Thamud and the evil people there. Prophet Salih ﷺ left the people saying, "Oh my people! I did indeed convey to you the message for which I was sent by my Lord: I gave you counsel, but you do not love good counselors." (7:79)

Once Salih ﷺ and his followers left, the remaining people realized that they had done a great wrong. The signs of Allah's ﷻ punishment began to appear. The faces of the people of Thamud began to turn yellow. The next day their faces began to turn red from fear. They knew that Allah's ﷻ punishment was coming.

After three days and nights, there came an earthquake that was so strong that it destroyed the town of Thamud and killed all the people there. Allah ﷻ had taught them a lesson. He had given them the camel as a sign of His power and they had still turned against Him.

Meanwhile, Prophet Salih ﷺ and his followers moved to another area where they could live and worship Allah ﷻ in peace and harmony.

About the Author

Suhaib Hamid Ghazi

Suhaib Ghazi was born in Boston, Massachusettes, but has grown up in California, Minnesota, Chicago, and Jeddah, Saudi Arabia. The author, who calls Chicago his home, is currently enrolled at the University of Redlands with his twin brother, Usam, in California, where he is pursuing Political Science and Business Administration as a double major. His future plans include attending Law School and perhaps even Business School.